AF422390

The Gospel of Mary

A Modern Commentary

Jeff Hood

The bold unitalicized words are the text.

All other text is commentary.

The numbers represent a way of numbering the comments according to text order.

The first part of the manuscript is missing. The existing text starts below...

. . . Will matter then be destroyed or not?

21

The fundamental question of human existence {.} Every letter is a longing to breathe. Every syllable is a longing to know. Every word is a longing to be. Will my matter matter? The question is born out of despair but bathed in hope. The answer will either

destroy or birth a new tomorrow. Mary is speaking for us

all...and we all wait with great anticipation for the Savior's reply.

Christ said, "All natures, all formations, all creatures

exist in and with one another,

22

Everything is connected. There is no separation between

anything. We are what we are. We are everything. We are

anything. We are.

and they will be resolved again into their own roots.

23

All things are collapsing into what is so that we might become

what was and what will ever be. The collapse into birth is

salvation. The collapse into creation is salvation. The collapse into God is salvation. The journey back is salvation.

For the nature of matter is resolved into the roots of its own nature.

24

Matter is slowly being released to return to the origin of matter...matter...the root of nature...God. The release of all that holds us back from the beginning is the beginning of redemption...the restoration of all.

Those who have ears to hear, let them hear!"

25

What about those who do not have ears? What about those who cannot hear? The exhortation goes much deeper than any physical characteristic. The exhortation is about one opening

their heart...regardless of their physical state. It is an invitation

to knowing...to being...to the epicenter of matter.

Peter said to Christ, "Since you have explained

everything to us, tell us this also:

31

It is human to long to know more. The problem with such

longing is that it can complicate that which we already

know...the root. Sometimes the answer to the question lies in the

question...and perhaps that is where our longing should most

generatively reside...being the question.

What is the sin of the world?"

32

Where did everything go wrong? Every civilization has sought to

answer the question. Perhaps the answer is that there is no

answer...there is only us.

Christ said, "There is no sin,

33

The idea of the nonexistence of sin is an invitation back to a

space of wholeness in being...a formative` place where there was

no sin.

but it is you who make sin when you do the things that

are like the nature of adultery, which is called sin.

34

We are the creators of the allusion of sin. Chaos enters our

matter because we run around on the matter that really matters.

Running around only makes you dizzy...unable to grasp hold of

who and what ultimately is.

That is why the Good came into your midst, to the

essence of every nature

35

Love is all that is good. Love came into our midst to lead us to

love...the core of who we are. We were brought forth from

love...we are being broken down to love...and we will return to

both or origin and our destiny...love. Love is all that is good.

in order to restore it to its root.

36

Love is the root. To pursue anything other than love is to deny

the root. We are nothing without the root.

Then He continued and said, "That is why you become

sick and die,

37

Sickness and death flow out of a denial of love. We have denied

the perfect and are left with the partial. The day is coming when

love will do away with anything that is partial. Love is the only

thing that can speed up such a process...the day when love will

be completely restored...will win.

for you love what deceives you.

38

Love can never be replaced. The seeker will always be searching until they do away with all that might deceive them and turn to love.

Let all who have a mind to understand, understand.

39

Partial understanding is not understanding. One must commit to understand that which they understand. How far will one go to grasp the fullness of understanding? It seems that it is worth everything.

Matter gives birth to a passion that has no equal, because it proceeds from something contrary to nature.

310

Our nature is love. Passion can corrupt such nature....because

passion can blinds us to what love really is...something that

never fails.

Then there arises a disturbance in its whole body.

311

Our bodies matter. Our matter matters. We cannot love the

neighbor until we love our body. Wholeness in our body is the

beginning of wholeness in all that is. Disturbances in our body

are a disturbance in all that is. Wholeness begins within the

body.

That is why I said to you, "You shall become satisfied,

and not persuaded. You shall be joined in the presence of

the likeness of nature.

312

What does it mean to become satisfied in love? What does it

mean to not be persuaded by passion? It means that you will be

joined with the likeness of nature...love.

Those who have ears to hear, let them hear."

313

Love. That is the matter upon which all matter rests. Listen.

When Christ said this, Christ greeted them all, saying,

"Peace be with you.

41

The blessed one always brings the peace. We are called to be the

blessed one. We become blessed when our matter connects to

the ground of matter...love.

Receive my peace unto yourselves.

42

Be the incarnation of love as Christ was the incarnation. Be love.

Be Christ.

Beware that no one lead you astray saying...

43

Cling to the teachings of love that you know are real within

you....surely nothing else will ever be as real as the impression

and expression of the root of your soul.

'Look here!' or 'Look there!'

44

There will be plenty who try all sorts of things to distract you from the work of love...resist with all that you are...for the integrity of your soul is at stake. There is nothing over here. There is nothing over there.

For Christ is within you.

45

This a beautiful description of the Christ. The incarnation is Child of God yet also Child of Humanity. So too can we be... We are made to be/in/of/through Christ. We are the Christ child.

Follow It!

46

Follow the Christ that is within you. There is no need to get saved...you have always been saved...Christ is within you...follow your salvation.

Those who seek will find.

47

Those willing to touch the Christ within will be able to grasp the Christ within.

Go then and preach the Good News of Christ.

48

One does not change the world by changing people...you change the world by sharing with them that the change is already within them. We are made in the image of the Christ. Salvation lives within us. Salvation for the world (even the cosmos) lives within us. Go to the realm and be liberators of the Christ!

Do not lay down any rules beyond what I appointed you,

49

Fuck the rules. Love Christ {.}

and do not give a law like the lawgiver, lest you be confined by it.

410

Rules are a prison that always imprison their creator first. Rules are death. Love is life. Live into the freedom of love that is within you.

When Christ said this, Christ departed.

411

The Christ declares that the Christ will never leave us nor

forsake us. How could the Christ? The Christ is within us all.

However, there are certainly tim0es where the Christ is more

real than others. Hold on to such times...for they are always the

starkest reminder of what is within.

But they were pained. They wept greatly, saying,

51

Hopelessness often births tears. When one has touched the root

of the Christ, they realize that there is no hope apart from it.

Despair can set in. Until, one realizes that hope remains

eternally embedded in the hope that remains within.

**"How shall we go to the world and preach the Gospel of
the Christ?**

52

The danger of the external Christ is it fosters a belief that one can
be alone. The internal Christ teaches us that we are never alone.
No one can stop the message of the Christ. Despite what is going
on around us, the Child of Humanity has already prepared us for
whatever is to come.

If they did not spare Christ, how will they spare us?"

53

Fear is not of Christ. Our prayer mustn't be to not be spared.
Our prayer must be that we follow the way of Christ.

Then Mary stood up, greeted them all, and said,

54

Mary is the inheritor of the mantle of Christ upon the ascension of Christ. History has tried to silence oppressed and marginalized peoples since the beginning of time...but Christ gives the mantle to Mary. The Christ within us will become most apparent when we unite our person to the marginalized and oppressed. Mary is one of the greatest embodiments of Christ to ever live...and she has not often been given her due because she had a vagina. She greets the disciples as their leader and we should treat her as such.

"Do not weep or grieve or doubt,

55

Death is synonymous with pain. Pain is synonymous with tears.

Tears are synonymous with doubt. But, they don't have to be.

The Christ calls us to not engage such things as those who are

without hope. There is freedom in knowing that Christ lives.

for Christ's grace will be with you and shelter you.

56

Grace is too often thought of as simply a pardon. In the realm of

the Christ, grace is a restoration...or as if nothing wrong ever

happened. Meaning, the shelter of grace is such that love always

wins. In the realm of love, the restoration never dies.

But rather, let us praise Christ's greatness,

57

Praise is too often thought of as fawning to the floor in awe.

Perhaps, praise is something much more...namely, love...or a way

of being complete in the presence of another. Praise is about

wholeness.

for Christ has prepared us and made us Human."

58

In all divine splendor, Christ created us to be human. In Christ,

we are most fully human. Perhaps in us, Christ is most fully

human as well.

When Mary said this, she turned their hearts to the

Good,

59

Turning toward the good is about turning toward the path of restoration...for there is nothing good apart from restoration. Turned hearts are restored hearts.

and they began to discuss the words of Christ.

510

The words of the Christ are most fully illuminated in discussion with the Christ. Surely, Christ bumping into Christ births more Christ...or illuminates the exponential nature of the Christ.

Peter said to Mary, "Sister we know that Christ loved you more than the rest of the women.

61

Peter can't make sense of Christ's love for Mary...so he has to qualify it amongst all the women. Truth be told, it is possible that Mary was closer to Christ than anyone else...not just amongst the women. Certainly, it is beyond possible that Mary was erased from most accounts.

Tell us the words of the Savior, which you remember, which you know but we do not...those that we have not heard."

62

Mary has something that the other disciples want...hidden knowledge. Christ manifests exponentially in those who create room for that which is hidden. Mary has created such room. The male disciples have not.

Mary answered and said, "What Christ has hidden from you I will tell you."

63

Despite the stifling patriarchy that surrounded her, Mary took

pity on the other disciples and granted their request. The nature

of the love of Christ is that it is not a collector or keeper of

wrongs...but rather a liberator of the Christ that is in us all.

And she began to speak to them Christ's words.

64

Deep within her humanity, Christ gives Mary the ability to put

into words that for which there is no words.

"I," she said, "I saw Christ in a vision

71

Christ grants the power of "I." When we are one with the Christ

within, we have the ability to declare who and what we are. The

"I" is a symbol of possession. "I" possess myself. "I" possess the Christ within. "I" had a vision...this is mine and out of the love of Christ within me..."I" am going to share it with you.

and I said to Christ, 'I saw you today in a vision.'

72

Mary engages the Christ again...not because Christ doesn't know that Mary saw the Christ...but rather to remind her self of what she saw. In the midst of this moment of vision, Mary keeps coaching her self to stay in/with the vision.

Christ answered and said to me, 'Blessed are you because you did not waver at the sight of Me.

73

Christ affirms Mary's persistence...and in doing so...lifts her up as

an example of the unwavering spirit that everyone should have.

Mary is keeping her mind right.

For where the mind is, there is the treasure.'

74

Mary's mind is concentrated on her treasure, the Christ. To

concentrate on anything else is not to concentrate on

treasure...but rather death.

I said to Christ, 'How does one who sees the vision see it,

through the soul or through the spirit?'

75

In asking the question, Mary wants to know about the soul and

the spirit. Which is most necessary to ascertain the things of

God? This is not just a question for the moment. Mary sees this question as the question of existence.

Christ answered and said, "One does not see through the Soul or Spirit,

76

Immediately, Christ rebukes the question entirely...to direct Mary to a secret higher truth.

but it is the mind between the two that sees the vision.'"

77

Unlike most other writings about the Christ, Mary is directed toward the mind as a means of salvation...perhaps not as the only means of salvation...but certainly an integral part of any transformation.

Major gap in manuscript...

"And Desire said,

91

Due to the fact that only incomplete manuscripts of the Gospel of Mary have been found, there is a huge gap in the text. The missing text appears to be partially or maybe even wholly a description of the Soul's ascension to God (the Soul seems to be referring to Christ's Soul). In the midst of this story, the text picks up.

Desire is one of the manifestations that is keeping the Soul from uniting fully with God.

'I did not see you descending, but now I see you ascending.

92

Desire speaks as if it is an old acquaintance the Soul. It speaks to the direction that the Soul is going. Desire is sure that it can stop the Soul from ascending to God.

Why do you lie since you belong to me?'

93

Desire clearly expresses a belief that it owns the Soul...and can do with it whatever it wishes. Thus is the nature of desire...

The Soul answered and said, 'I saw you. You did not see me or recognize me.

94

The Soul basically replies that it has been looking out for Desire.

The Soul has prepared for this meeting.

I served you as a garment

95

The garment speaks of the Soul's shell...i.e. what Desire thought

it saw it didn't see because it wasn't looking deeply or beyond

the Soul's garment or shell.

and you did not know me.'

96

Everybody/Desire thinks they really know somebody...know

their heart...and most of the time they don't have a clue. The

Soul is declaring that Desire never took the time to actually look

at the Soul. i.e. "You don't know me!"

When the Soul said this, it went away rejoicing greatly.

97

The Soul escaped the trap of Desire by being most authentically

the Soul.

Again it came to the third power, which is called

Ignorance.

98

In numbering the power, the passage illustrates that Ignorance is one of many ascent obstacles the Soul faces.

The power questioned the Soul, saying, 'Where are you going?

99

Ignorance is like a guard demanding to know where a trespasser is going. The question is as much of a demand to stop as it is a question.

In wickedness are you enslaved.

910

Often...in our ignorance...we name things before they can name us. Wickedness named without is wickedness denied within.

You are chained...

911

Ignorance declares the Soul to be so wicked that the Soul can't

even name Ignorance's wickedness....i.e. you can't even begin to

talk about me.

do not judge!'

912

Ignorance declares the Soul to be in no position to judge so that

Ignorance doesn't have to face judgment.

And the Soul said, 'Why do you judge me since I have not

judged?

913

Preemptive judgment is one of the foremost tools of Ignorance. The Soul resists the temptation.

I was chained, though I have not chained.

914

Ignorance declares rule over the Soul and gives the Soul no opportunity to challenge such rule.

I was not recognized. But I have recognized that all matter is being dissolved, both the earthly things and the heavenly.'

915

Regardless, the Soul knows more than Ignorance. The Soul knows that all things are being freed...you can't simply imprison someone by calling them wicked anymore. Earth and Heaven are uniting to push back against such Ignorance. All is being made free.

When the Soul had overcome the third power, it went upwards and saw the fourth power,

916

Ignorance can never beat...or even respond to...freedom. The Soul moved onward toward freedom.

it took seven forms.

917

There are seven forms that the Soul had to respond to.

The first form is Darkness,

918

Darkness is that which obscures the Light...which is the eternal

guide.

the second Desire,

919

Desire is that which disorients the Path...which can confuse the

senses.

the third Ignorance,

920

Ignorance is that which blurs the Knowledge...which can distract

the mind.

the fourth is the Eagerness for Death,

921

Eagerness for Death can destroy Eagerness for Life.

the fifth is the Realm of the Flesh,

922

Realm of the Flesh can destroy hunger for the Realm of the

Eternal.

the sixth is the Foolish Wisdom of Flesh,

923

Foolish Wisdom of the Flesh can distract from Eternal Wisdom of the Soul.

the seventh is the Wrathful Wisdom.

924

Wrathful Wisdom is the opposite of the Wisdom of Grace.

These are the Seven Powers of Wrath.

925

The informed Soul knows that the seven Powers of Wrath will never be any match for the beauty of Grace.

They asked the Soul, 'Where are you coming from human-killer, or where are you going, place-destroyer?'

926

By labeling the Soul as a human-killer and place-destroyer, the

Seven Powers are trying to confuse the Soul into thinking that

the complete Restoration of all things is no longer a reality.

The Soul answered and said, 'What binds me has been

slain, and what turns me about has been destroyed, and

my desire has been filled, and my ignorance is dead.

927

Rules are dead. Grace reigns. Eternal focus rules. Death is dead.

Righteousness abounds. Evil has been washed away.

Knowledge is complete. Ignorance is dead. The Soul is being

completely restored.

In a world I was released from a world, and in a mold from a higher mold, and from the chain of forgetfulness...which is temporal.

928

The Soul has been released from time and space so that the Soul might fully be time and space...all knowledge now belongs to the Soul. The chain of destruction is finished. The Soul will never die. Holiness is eternally holy.

From this second on, I will attain the rest of time, of the season, of the generations, I well rest content.'"

929

In Silence, the Soul waits until the restoration is complete...leaving only the Soul's path/light to guide all that might come after.

When Mary said this, she fell silent,

930

Mary waited in the Silence with the Soul until the vision was

complete.

since it was to this point that Christ had spoken with her.

931

After the Way of the Savior was expressed, there was a heaviness

that came over the room.

But Andrew answered and said, "Say what you want

about what she has said.

101

Andrew thinks he knows the Christ better than anyone else.

Fundamentalism takes us to places where we close our ears.

Fundamentalism causes to miss the Christ.

I do not believe that the Christ said this. For certainly these teachings are strange ideas.

102

I do not believe... The passage could end there. The point is that Andrew doesn't believe anyone beyond Andrew. We have to get over our hesitancies to embrace the strange...the Queer...the Christ.

Peter answered and spoke concerning these same things. He questioned them: "Did Christ really speak privately with a woman without us knowing about it?

103

Can you imagine if someone responded by saying, "Did he really speak with a man without our knowing about it?"? Of course not...which is why it is abundantly clear that Peter is discounting the teachings of the Christ simply because they are being shared with him by someone who has a vagina...Mary.

Are we to turn about and all listen to her? Did Christ prefer her to us?"

104

The truth drops. Peter...and the rest of the men...are scared that the Christ might have chosen a woman over them. Male fragility cannot silence the Christ.

Then Mary wept and said to Peter, "My brother Peter, what do you think?

105

Mary begs Peter to believe her. Why would she lie? Peter is stunned by her conviction. I guess he thought she was just going to step aside. However, the Christ never steps aside.

Do you think that I have thought this up myself in my heart, or that I am lying about the Christ?

106

Mary will not get off of it. This is her truth for the world...and she is not going to let anyone deny it. The Christ has been revealed and she is not going back in the closet...for this is the day of salvation...this is the day of the Christ.

Levi answered and said to Peter, "Peter you have always been an angry person.

107

Levi wants to be found with Christ. In the teachings of Mary, he has found the Christ once more. Nobody is going to turn him around.

Now I see you contending against the woman like the adversary.

108

Peter's sexism is dramatically challenged. Levi laughs at him for throwing around his masculinity as if it has the weight of divine revelation. Christ alone...and nothing else.

But if the Savior made her worthy, who are you to reject her?

109

Mary teaches us that it is Christ who does the incarnating...not us...so look for Christ...not the desired places that you would hope to see Christ.

Surely the Christ knows her very well. That is why He loved her more than us.

110

Christ is trustworthy...Christ choose Mary...Mary becomes trustworthy...Mary becomes Christ. The incarnation of the Christ keeps happening incessantly. Christ choose Mary because Christ knew that she would pass the teachings on so that they might become Christ for others. Christ loved Mary because Christ knew that Mary would joyfully share the teachings of the Christ...and never stop loving all she would find along the way.

Rather let us be ashamed and put on the perfect, and become righteous as Christ commanded us

111

In the midst of it all, Levi feels shame...shame that the gathered are about to miss the Christ because they can't see past their dicks. In this moment, Levi demands that they put on the Christ...and engage the situation as they know the Christ would.

and preach the gospel,

112

The Christ...the incarnate God who loves us...is the forever good news. Levi demands that the gathered realize that the teachings of Mary are good news. There is no reason to sit and argue about them any longer. Simply, go out and use them to take Christ to the world.

not laying down any other rule or other law beyond what Christ said."

113

Earlier, Andrew tried to lay down the law. Earlier, Peter tried to lay down the law. Earlier, they were all trying to lay down the law and not listening with their hearts. There is but one law of Christ...that of love. Nothing else matters. Mary knew that and that is the power of her message.

After he said these things, they started going out to teach and proclaim.

114

Emboldened, Mary and Levi left to share the love of Christ.

Surely, there is no greater calling.

The Gospel according to Mary.

115

The Gospel of Mary is good news for all that are willing to embrace the power of love. There is liberation here...if we can get over our selves long enough to experience it.